It's a Dad's Thing

PART 2 - THE CRUEL DAD

ADAM ATCHA

Balboa Press books may be ordered through booksellers or by contacting:

Balboa Press
A Division of Hay House
1663 Liberty Drive
Bloomington, IN 47403
www.balboapress.com.au
AU TFN: 1 800 844 925 (Toll Free inside Australia)
AU Local: 0283 107 086 (+61 2 8310 7086 from outside Australia)

ISBN: 978-1-5043-2299-7 (sc)
ISBN: 978-1-5043-2300-0 (e)

Print information available on the last page.

Balboa Press rev. date: 10/21/2020

BALBOAPRESS
A DIVISION OF HAY HOUSE

An Authoritarian Dad is
Relaxed and Spontaneous –

A Humble Dad wants Her or
Him or Both to love through
Wisdom and Respect

A Courageous Dad endures
a disciplined Mind in the
Harshest Situation for him or
her to Witness Bravery –

A Cuddly Dad wants more Hugs
and Kisses for reassurance –

A Trustworthy Dad never or
seldomly lies to Her or Him

A Workaholic Dad wants
Him to love through an
Academic point of View so
He can love Him thereafter.

A Coward Dad loves His
Wife more than himself

An Immature Dad is somewhat
cruel without any intentional
Harm and is unaware of
His own Behaviour –

A Romantic Dad wants to
love Her through Everything
he sees, smells…

A Jealous Dad wants Her to only
love Him and nobody Else –

A High Roller Dad becomes a
Faithful mother to Him and Her

A Fit Dad wants to impress
Through a healthy Lifestyle –

An Abusive Dad never
hurts Her/Him –

A Lonely Dad only needs
Him and Her –

An emotional Dad wants constant
Approval and Affection

A Cunning Dad wants Her/
Him to Hate his Enemies –

A good Father does not Care –

A Mature Dad knows
everything she Knows
naturally – Mind Flowing

An ignorant dad knows She/
Him Trusts you most yet
cannot see it yet needs Proof.

A Heartbroken Dad loves
Her/Him through his
Pain and Suffering

Printed in the United States
By Bookmasters